Luiz Carlos Martins Loyola Filho

Score reading with the O Passo method

Luiz Carlos Martins Loyola Filho

Score reading with the O Passo method

A study on reading rhythms with primary school teachers

ScienciaScripts

Cover image: www.ingimage.com

This book is a translation from the original published under ISBN 978-3-330-76733-1.

Publisher:
Sciencia Scripts
is a trademark of
Dodo Books Indian Ocean Ltd. and OmniScriptum S.R.L publishing group

120 High Road, East Finchley, London, N2 9ED, United Kingdom
Str. Armeneasca 28/1, office 1, Chisinau MD-2012, Republic of Moldova, Europe
Managing Directors: Ieva Konstantinova, Victoria Ursu
info@omniscriptum.com

Printed at: see last page
ISBN: 978-620-8-56648-7

ACKNOWLEDGEMENTS

First of all, I thank God for the gift of life and free will, and for loving me regardless of my mistakes, blessing me, giving me health and disposition, my family and colleagues. I thank the Lord for music and for inspiring me every day.

To my supervisor Rosane Cardoso de Araújo, whom I affectionately call my "academic mother", because she is the person who has played a fundamental role in my career, motivating me from the beginning to research and strengthen music education.

To my family, especially my mum, Mirian, my dad, Luiz Carlos, and my brother, Gabriel, for always supporting me in my choices and welcoming me at all times.

To Fabiana, for pushing me to be better. For all my learning and support in life and in my projects.

To Lucas Ciavatta, for sharing his knowledge and experience.

To Professors Cristiane Otutumi and Ana Paula Peters for their pertinent and enriching guidance.

To Professor Jean, for all his attention, care and willingness.

To the research participants who helped make this study possible.

To CAPES, for the financial support that enabled me to carry out this research with great dedication.

The way your heart beats makes all the
difference in learning to live

John Myung - Dream Theater

Score reading with the O Passo method: a study of rhythm reading with primary school teachers

This book presents my master's thesis entitled "A study on the development of rhythmic reading at first sight using the O Passo method". Music reading is considered valuable for learning and practising music, especially for promoting the student's musical autonomy. Musicians display different levels of this skill, and this becomes more evident when reading at first sight, in which the primary source of information is the score. References in the field of music reading indicate that sight-reading seems to be strongly related to rhythmic abilities, and that rhythmic reading ability is the main predictor of performance in a music reading task. For these reasons, the focus of this research is on rhythmic sight-reading based on the O Passo method, with an emphasis on the O Passo score, the aim of which is to introduce traditional score decoding processes. The aim of this research was to investigate, by means of a quasi-experimental study, among other tools, the process of rhythmic sight-reading mediated by the O Passo method, while also observing the students' motivation throughout the research. Students were selected from a music teacher training course for basic education in the city of Curitiba-PR. The data collected indicates success rates of 40 per cent for the pre-test and 90 per cent for the post-test. The participants also answered questionnaires at the beginning and end of the research, and through these it was possible to see that the O Passo method contributed to their motivation in rhythmic reading tasks, as well as to their training as music teachers.

Keywords: Music - Rhythm; Rhythmic Reading; The Step Method.

SUMMARY

CHAPTER 1 5

CHAPTER 2 8

CHAPTER 3 13

CHAPTER 4 24

CHAPTER 5 30

CHAPTER 6 42

CHAPTER 1

Introduction

Research indicates that reading music is considered a valuable activity for learning and practising music, with the ability to promote student autonomy (BOYLE, 1970; CIAVATTA, 2009; FIREMAN, 2010). However, it can be seen that musicians have different levels of this skill, and this is even more evident when reading is done at first sight (LPV[1]), in which the primary source of information is the score (SLOBODA, 2006).

According to Boyle (1970), individuals who don't read at first sight have their musical experiences limited, and what is observed about LPV is that, in many contexts, its teaching and training is neglected, its necessity is questioned and it is often excluded from musical objectives, whether educational and/or performative (SLOBODA, 2008; FIREMAN, 2003; HOLLINGSWORTH, 2014).

When I came across music reading tasks at first glance (at least at a moderate level of complexity/difficulty), especially as a music degree student, I realised that I had a hard time solving them. My primary source for assimilating musical information has always been memorisation, i.e. prior knowledge of the piece of music in question. This memorisation, in turn, took place mainly through listening (auditory input). Therefore, if I didn't have the means to listen to it, reading would suffer.

My main involvement with the score was therefore using it as a guide for a piece of music that I had already memorised. This type of use of the score considerably limited my musical experiences and also affected my motivation for reading music, and for this reason among others I realised a need to value this activity. According to Persellin (1992), this is due to the fact that my preference and style of musical memorisation was based mainly on the auditory modality, rather than the visual or kinaesthetic modalities.

The choice of this topic also arose from my experience with the O Passo method, which, through its principles, bases, tools and concepts, provided me with answers, especially to questions about rhythm and music reading, which arose during my degree in Music, in my activity as a guitar and guitar teacher for 14 years, as a guitarist and guitarist in various contexts, and also as a primary school teacher. Remembering some of the experiences I've had with students with great rhythmic difficulties, I've come to believe that I have a "gift" for rhythm. But with the O Passo method, I experienced a systematised way of using body movements to develop musical skills, including rhythmic reading. In addition to the auditory modality, today I consider the kinaesthetic and visual modalities not only as possibilities, but also as essential for any musical activity.

In addition to Ciavatta's work with the O Passo method, I recognise here the work of other method

[1] In this paper, the English term sightreading and its abbreviation SR, found in the references of this research, have been replaced by their Portuguese relative, leitura à primeira vista (LPV).

authors, as stated by Simão (2013),

> It is important to remember the thinkers and researchers who conceived activities with body movements that are inseparable from making music, because they built the foundations of music education in the 20th century. We should mention Emile Jaques-Dalcroze, Carl Orff, Theophil Maier, Murray Schafer and Hans Joachin Koellreutter (SIMÃO, 2013, p. 21) for the relevance of their work to music, both in the traditional form and in creative experiments in music education.

I would also highlight Brazilian music education authors and methodologies in the fields of rhythm and musical perception, such as the work carried out by the Barbatuques group (SIMÃO, 2013), and especially the authors of the methodologies I came into contact with during my degree, such as Heitor Pozzoli and José Eduardo Gramani. I believe that a dialogue between O Passo and other methodologies can be enriching for different perspectives. However, the objectives and literature review of this work will not be extended in this direction.

Returning to music reading, research indicates that it is strongly related to rhythmic skills (LEHMANN AND MCARTHUR, 2002), with rhythmic reading skills being the main predictor of performance in reading tasks (BOYLE, 1970; ELLIOT, 1982; BEBEAU, 1982; SHEHAN, 1987; MCPHERSON, 1994).

Another point to be made here is the indication of the effectiveness of using body movements to teach reading, especially rhythmic reading (BOYLE, 1970; BEBEAU, 1982), as well as highlighting methods that use other forms of rhythmic notation - such as phonemes, syllables, letters, numbers, words, etc. - to decode traditional score notation (BEBEAU, 1982; COLLEY, 1987; ESTER, SHEIB AND INKS, 2006; CIAVATTA, 2009).

The general aim of this research is based on the elements outlined in this introduction: to investigate the process of rhythmic reading at first sight mediated by the O Passo method with a group of students on a music teacher training course for basic education. To this end, the research will be guided by specific objectives, which are: to analyse the reading level of the participants before and after the activities with the method; and to verify, from the participants' point of view, their motivation in using the O Passo method to learn rhythmic reading at first sight. The choice of the group of second degree students is justified by the fact that they will be teaching music in mainstream schools, and the way in which these individuals deal with the subject of musical reading in this context is highly relevant to this research.

In order to develop this study, I firstly review music reading and reading at first sight, in which we consider the activity, its characteristics and complexity. Next, I present a brief explanation of rhythmic reading, in which we consider this skill. The next chapter presents the O Passo method, its tools and concepts that are introduced into music teaching. Continuing the theoretical bibliographical review, the chapter on motivation for musical learning presents studies and theories on this psychological aspect, currently a sub-area of psychology, initially in a general way, i.e. applicable to any activity, and later on education, music education and performance. Next, in the Methodology chapter, I present the method, the data collection instruments, the context in which the research was carried out and the stages of the investigation. The results of the data collected are then analysed in the light of the theoretical framework. Finally, the conclusions and final considerations are presented, in which discussions and implications for future studies on the subject are proposed.

The aim of this research is to propose and demonstrate to those involved in music education and practice the value of reading as a resource for the individual's musical autonomy, as well as strategies and tools that can help and motivate students to learn rhythm and the traditional score, more specifically rhythmic notation, and which can consequently contribute to the development of musical reading at first sight.

CHAPTER 2

MUSICAL READING

Music reading is the interpretation of musical ideas (defined by information on rhythm, pitch, expression, etc.) represented by conventional and specific signs (musical codes) contained in a score (RAMOS E MARINO, 2003; CIAVATTA, 2009). According to Sloboda (2004), this activity is also considered a type of musical perception, but the perceived object (input) is visual and not auditory.

Reading a score is a task that is present in various musical contexts - whether educational or performative, whether for learning and rehearsing a piece, or for later guiding the performance of that piece, among others. According to Ramos and Marino, "writing and reading music are part of the process of learning music and become essential for mastering and understanding this language" (RAMOS E MARINO, 2003, p.44). According to Ciavatta (2009), the ability to represent musical ideas through notation is a tool for musical independence. According to Boyle (1970), the ability to read music has long been recognised as a valuable tool with which students can broaden their musical experiences.

For Fireman (2010),

> In practical terms, reading makes it possible for a composer to be remembered for his works and for them to be interpreted again without time limits. Performance preparation time can be reduced and the instrumentalist will have more time to devote to interpretative aspects. Reading gives us the chance to glimpse different cultures, concepts, places, sensations, feelings and more. You can establish new mental representations of aspects you already know and establish relationships and organised structures (p. 18)

Considering the characteristics of music reading pointed out by the authors, we realise that the possibilities it can provide are enriching for musical activities. For this reason, this chapter will look at two aspects of music reading: firstly sight-reading and then rhythmic reading.

2.1 Reading at first sight (LPV)

According to Sloboda (2008), musicians have different levels of music reading skills. Even competent musicians with a high level of musical knowledge may have low levels of music reading, while others may have excellent levels of this skill. In this sense, the author states that the task that most strongly highlights these differences is reading at first sight (LPV), and adds that this is a "cleaner" and "simpler" case of reading, in which the performance is not "contaminated" with long-term knowledge of the piece of music in question.

According to Sloboda, LPV is a task that contrasts with one in which the score is used only as a guide in the performance of music that has already been learnt (memorised). In the latter, long-term memory is the primary source of information about the music, not the score. But the author goes on to say that, obviously, long-term memory (in which general musical knowledge is stored) is also implicit in LPV, just as knowledge of language, verbal and written, is for reading a text.

According to Penttinen and Huovinen (2011), research on LPV has traditionally focused on explaining and/or predicting general reading skills at first sight based on other factors. The authors argue that these factors include:

1) Instruction methods;
2) Specific musical skills such as remembering written music or the ability to read rhythm at a glance;
3) Performance in (general) reading or maths, as well as more general skills such as spatial-temporal reasoning;
4) Recognising visual patterns;
5) Cognitive styles.

The authors also point out that there is currently a growing consensus that performance on the LPV can be predicted by multiple perceptual, cognitive and motor skills, which can be partly related to practice and partly unrelated to practice.

According to Kopiez and Lee (2006), LPV "is not only of particular interest to musical occupations such as pianists, conductors [...], but is also one of the five basic[2] performance skills that every musician must acquire" (p. 97). According to Lehmann and McArthur (2002), LPV is an indispensable part of any serious testing and subsequent training for musicians.

Sloboda (2008) and Lehmann, Sloboda and Woody (2007) state that LPV is proof that the individual has conceptually mastered the musical system. Boyle (1970) states that individuals who do not read at first sight have limited musical experiences. In this sense, a number of researchers have investigated the characteristics of the processes for developing this skill (BOYLE, 1970; LEHMANN and MCARTHUR; 2002; KOPIEZ and LEE, 2006; LEHMANN, SLOBODA and WOODY, 2007; FIREMAN, 2007; SLOBODA, 2008; COSTA, 2011; OTUTUMI, 2011).

What is commonly observed in relation to LPV is that, in many contexts, it seems to be excluded from the objectives of those involved in music education and practice. According to Sloboda (2008), there are modern educational techniques that seem to bypass LPV. One widely used strategy for solving a task that initially requires score reading is memorisation, "so that the performance doesn't depend on reading skills"

[2] 1) Playing rehearsed music; 2) Playing by sight-reading music; 3) Playing "from memory"; 4) Playing "by ear"; and 5) Improvising (McPherson, 1995).

(SLOBODA, 2008, p. 88).

According to Fireman (2007) and also Hollingsworth (2014), as it is not an essential skill for making music or being a musician, its teaching and training is often neglected by schools, and some experts question its necessity. In a broader context, Ciavatta (2009) states that

> [...] many musicians with intense and consistent practice don't use graphic notation and don't even consider it an issue. [...]. But then who considers the use of graphic notation an issue? Possibly both those who don't write [don't read] and clearly realise the limitation that this can mean, and those who write [read] and still don't solve a series of problems in their musical practice. (CIAVATTA, 2009, p. 74).

However, theorists claim that the exclusion of LPV from music-educational objectives is due to the fact that it is considered a very difficult task, to the point that many musicians agree that "the performer who has the courage to go on stage without prior knowledge of the pieces to be played is a hero" (SLOBODA, 2008, p.88). Research in this direction indicates that a large number of musicians attribute this skill as innate or requiring great effort to acquire (LEHMANN & MCARTHUR, 2002; SLOBODA, 2008; FIREMAN, 2007; COSTA, 2011).

This difficulty seems to be associated with the complexity and demands of the task. Researchers claim that performing sight-reading requires a great deal of processing of highly complex visual information (the score) without the possibility of error correction and under real-time constraints (KOPIEZ and LEE, 2006). According to Lehmann and McArthur (2002), LPV is made up of sub-skills that occur simultaneously and which, from a psychological point of view, are:

1) Perception (decoding note patterns);
2) Kinaesthesia (execution of motor plans);
3) Memorisation (pattern recognition);
4) Ability to solve problems (improvising and guessing).

Still on the complexity and demands of the LPV task, Otutumi (2011) explains the relationship between reading at first sight and memory, stating that in order for a musician to be identified as a more proficient reader, they must seek the smallest gap between the reading of the piece and the rehearsed performance (memorised). According to the author, the minimum that is required in an LPV activity is for the reader to leave aside the mere deciphering of notes, performing the piece with reasonable tempo and expression.

Corroborating this, Mishra (2014) attests, with the results of his research into factors related to the accuracy of sight-reading, that LPV is considered a musical skill that develops alongside the performer's musicality rather than as a process of visual-motor decoding.

Researchers also point to the fact that individuals don't receive proper training in reading throughout their formative years (LEHMANN and MCARTHUR, 2002; SLOBODA, 2008; FIREMAN, 2007; COSTA, 2011; WINTER and SINICO, 2012). Sloboda (2008), comparing language reading to LPV, observes the fact that language reading is necessary for a complete involvement with our culture, but the same does not happen with music, and that LPV is therefore not taught rigorously and does not occur so early in children's development. According to Fireman (2007), some perceptions and guidelines are often observed in music education contexts, such as those in the following extract:

> Either it is believed that it will come over time and that few will be given the "gift", or sometimes students are recommended to read as much as they can so that they develop the skill simply by being involved in the activity (FIREMAN, 2007, p. 32).

Looking at the considerations of the authors reviewed on the activity of reading music, at first glance one realises that it is a complex subject with many factors/variables involved. This fact also led to the research objectives being cut back to deal only with rhythmic reading.

2.2 Rhythmic reading

According to Cooper and Meyer (1963), to study rhythm is to study the whole of music, because, according to them, rhythm is more than a mere sequence of proportions of duration, but rather the intimate and intrinsic interaction of temporal organisation with all the other processes and forces that form music, organising and being organised by them. According to Hasty (1997), music can be defined as the "rhythmisation" of sound.

Hodges cites Drake's research (apud HODGES, 1992), in which a highly positive correlation was observed between rhythmic performance and general performance in musical skills. According to Hodges, the relationship between music reading and rhythmic reading provided the only correlations with coefficients high enough to indicate rhythmic reading ability as a predictor of LPV performance.

According to Shehan (1987), the difficulty of accurately reading rhythms in the score is a frequent cause of difficulty in reading music, both for beginners and experienced musicians. According to the author, although many instruments can produce pitches without the need to internalise them, rhythmic reading requires auditory coding.

Elliot (1982), in his research into the relationship between instrumental sight-reading and predictor variables , states that the results of his research indicate a strongly positive relationship between LPV and the ability to read rhythmic patterns at first sight. The author also states that the results of his research corroborate the argument that regular practice of reading rhythmic patterns tends to be beneficial for improving LPV.

Gary McPherson (1994), in his study on factors and skills that influence LPV ability, assessed the sight-reading of 101 students using a performance scale. According to the author, the results showed that rhythmic errors outnumbered all others, and he concludes that the results of his study suggest that efficient LPV depends largely on the musician's ability to read and understand rhythm.

Boyle (1970), in his research into the effect of prescribing rhythmic movements on sight-reading skills, suggests that rhythmic reading and sight-reading have a high degree of relationship, and that the use of rhythmic body movements can contribute to the acquisition of rhythmic reading, music reading and sight-reading skills.

According to Bebeau (1982), studies on rhythmic reading are important because the main source of errors in LPV is the inability to read rhythmic patterns. According to the author, a prerequisite for teaching rhythmic reading is the acquisition of the ability to maintain a regular pulse, and music educators generally agree that this acquisition should preferably take place through physical (bodily/kinesthetic) activities. According to the author, rhythm reading is a difficult skill to acquire, and one of the reasons for this difficulty is that traditional methods require the acquisition of mathematical concepts before they can be used, demanding concentration and a considerable amount of cognitive processing. Another issue with the traditional method pointed out by the author is that if the individual doesn't concentrate hard on maintaining the pulse, they may be tempted to merely approximate the duration value represented in the symbols.

Lehmann and McArthur (2002) indicate strategies to remedy common problems in sight-reading pitch, rhythm, articulation and expression with a) the isolated practice of these parameters, b) the use of technical equipment, c) strategic preparations for performance. With regard to rhythmic reading, the same authors indicate strategies for its development. These are:

1) Play the rhythm by clapping (or with other forms of rhythmic body movements);
2) Writing counts in the score;
3) Draw vertical lines, which indicate the alignment of the notes;
4) Practising reading aided by a metronome or a device with MIDI playback such as a sequencer; and
5) Playing in an accompaniment or ensemble practice situation with real performers.

Taking these strategies into account, as well as the other considerations mentioned above about rhythm and rhythmic reading, it was possible to establish associations with the musical education method O Passo, to which the next chapter of this dissertation is dedicated.

CHAPTER 3

THE STEP

According to Lessa (2015) Passo can be considered an active method of music education because its experiences promote a direct experience with music by working with the body. In addition, the method follows the idea of music educators from the early 20th century that musical knowledge is something that should be offered to everyone, and not to a select minority of talented people.

According to Lucas Ciavatta[3] (2009), creator of the method, O Passo was created in 1996 and is, first and foremost, a tool for the construction of knowledge, which "works with the construction of a base, something that brings countless possibilities and opens a door, not only to rhythms and sounds, but to rhythm as a whole and to a real approach to the universe of sound" (p. 15).

According to Machado (2015), "the power of the O Passo method in regular schools [basic education] is not only explained by the methodology it proposes, but by the teaching philosophy it pursues, which brings it closer to the field of education and at the same time universalises it" (p. 32). Frank Abrahams (apud CIAVATTA, 2009) states that although the method is focused on Brazilian rhythms, its principles can be used with the rhythms and melodies of any culture. Machado (2015) believes that,

> This strong characteristic of the method is justified by a solid conceptualisation of the principles and pillars that govern working with The Step. Knowing the method necessarily means familiarising yourself with these concepts. On the contrary, if we empty it of its principles and pillars, it becomes more of a collection of exercises than an actual method (p. 32).

Considering Machado's (2015) statement about the importance of these elements of the method, as well as my commitment as a researcher and music educator to get to know and review these fundamentals in order to enrich this dissertation, due attention will be paid to them here.

3.1 Principles of The Step

The principles of O Passo are considerations that seem to me to permeate areas such as philosophy and ethics. The two basic principles that govern O Passo are inclusion and autonomy. With regard to inclusion, Ciavatta (2009) states that every method should have this guideline, and that perhaps, in general, all methods aim to achieve this. Ciavatta cites Dalcroze (apud CIAVATTA, 2009), who, at the time [1967], proposed the "elimination of the incurable", in the same way that a blind man would be excluded from a shooting lesson.

---

[3] Lucas Ciavatta, a musician with a degree from UNIRIO and a Master's in Education from UFF, is the creator of the O Passo music education method. He is the director of the Instituto d'O Passo and the percussion and singing group Bloco d'O Passo.

According to Ciavatta, this statement is clearly a reflection of a historical context and Dalcroze himself would probably not allow such a statement. However, the author continues, even though today the vast majority of music educators are clearly against this attitude, O Passo's concern is also with how much is done, not only to prevent this "removal of the incurable", but "mainly so that those students who remain don't feel incurable and, over time, give up, 'remove' themselves (p. 19). In short, no one is completely free, no matter how good they think they are, from receiving this unfortunate label, the author emphasises.

With inclusion as its principle, The Step considers that nothing, no skill or understanding, should be taken for granted. According to the author, one of the great strengths of O Passo is precisely that it is based on a natural resource of any human being in ordinary conditions: walking, but that even this resource must be relearned "just like someone who goes to a Tai Chi class and needs to relearn how to breathe, to become aware of how they breathe in order to breathe better" (CIAVATTA, 2009, p. 19-20).

Then, considering his vision of inclusion, the author explains that:

> Our presence simply doesn't guarantee this inclusion. It is essential that this presence is accompanied by action and that it is significant for the group, that it interferes, positively or negatively, in the group's outcome. Ideally, it should be positive, because this interference will be increasingly desired and we will feel more and more part of the group. But even when it is negative, the important thing is that we will be noticed, and this can open up an excellent opportunity for us to be helped, to review our practice and to start interfering positively and really be part of that group (ibid., p. 20).

Passo is also concerned with a factor of exclusion which, especially in Brazil, must be viewed with all the seriousness it indicates: having or not having the means, i.e. any and all material resources whose absence, in some cases, makes the teaching/learning process unfeasible. For example, if a methodology is based on a piano, and the piano is not available, the approach will be unfeasible. The Pitch is therefore worked on

> Always from the perspective of the almost total absence of means (which, even in abundance, can be a very important exercise), relying only on those who want to teach/learn, those who want to learn/teach and the resources available for both (something very simple to do for those who have no other option). I work at O Passo today more and more from the perspective that the only resources really necessary to carry out a music education process are just clapping and voice; rhythm and sound in the only instruments whose presence we can actually guarantee (CIAVATTA, 2009, p. 20).

This corroborates the idea that O Passo is focused on building a foundation, because even the instruments needed are the most elementary. According to my understanding of the method, the development of the musical skills for which it was proposed is valid for any instrument.

Regarding autonomy, the second principle of O Passo, Lucas Ciavatta illustrates that "it is possible to spend your whole life in a percussion group and not have precise rhythmic references; that it is possible to sing your whole life in a choir and fall out of tune incredibly often" (ibidem, p. 21). The author continues his reasoning as follows,

> How can someone be in close and prolonged contact with a particular activity and not master the basic skills that this activity requires? [...]basically the solution to this mystery, to this apparent impossibility, lies in a word that negates the whole objective that I'm evoking here for The Step: "dependence". To depend entirely on the other (not to be confused with "relying on the other") is what those who play or sing always do a little later than those who know the right time and note, and can therefore give the impression (even to themselves) that they don't miss a beat or tune. But being dependent, being aware of your dependence, being purposefully "on the edge", is something only desired by those who at that moment have no other option, either because they don't have the strength or because they don't have the means. The means Passo provides, the strength usually comes from the realisation that through these means there is a real possibility of learning (ibidem, p. 21).

Ciavatta says that building this autonomy is necessarily linked to the rigour of those who assess, and warns that "rigour" should never be confused with "rigidity", because to be rigid is to be insensitive to diversity, while to be rigorous is not to protect anyone from their own ignorance. The author attests that the teacher who protects his student from his own ignorance is condemning that student to remain in the ignorance in which he finds himself.

Taking into account my experience as a teacher, I believe that these are essential principles for any educational activity, and that the teacher plays a fundamental role in balancing these principles with the educational objectives to be achieved. With this clear in mind, other characteristic aspects of the method, the pillars of The Step, are presented.

3.2 Pillars of The Step

The pillars of the method are: a) body, b) representation, c) group and d) culture. The following sections will review these aspects. Firstly, the body.

a) Body

About the body and music, I find that

> We all move when we play or sing. Moving while playing is inevitable, not least because the body is the only instrument we can't do without to make music. Any sound production that comes from a human being necessarily involves some bodily movement (CIAVATTA, 2009, p. 23).

According to the author, even if involuntarily, our body moves whenever we make music, altering and defining our musical realisation. Therefore, a move towards the relationship between body movement and musical movement is necessary, which is why The Step focuses on "the importance of the body for the acquisition of musical skills and understanding" (ibid., p.23).

The author then presents the relationship between bodily movement and the dimensions of space and time. Maffioletti (apud CIAVATTA, 2009) states that if the individual does not have experiences of space and time in order to integrate the notions of these dimensions, it will not be possible to internalise and learn about the outside world and, consequently, there will be motor, perceptual and cognitive disorganisation and uncoordination. Ciavatta (2009) states that the notions of space and time are constructed at the level of representation through bodily experience. For the author, there doesn't seem to be the possibility of an absence of the body in the realisation of this process, but what there may be is an under-utilisation of the body and a consequent under-development of these notions. He also emphasises that "experiences of space and time" depend entirely on a child's ability to learn with their own body.

Maffioletti (apud CIAVATTA, 2009) emphasises the importance of developing the notions of space and time for making music: "The perception of rhythms includes both the notion of time and space. Space-time organisation underpins rhythmic experiences" (MAFFIOLETTI apud CIAVATTA, 2009, p. 25).

From this statement it can be seen that

> The same individual who begins to explore time and space with their body necessarily does so within a rhythm (however irregular their movement, there is always a rhythm), and the more this individual knows what is being done rhythmically, the more they know the musical movements that are being suggested, the musical space that is being travelled, the more this individual's knowledge of their body, and their body in space and time, expands (CIAVATTA, 2009, p. 25).

In this approach, the body is seen as a knowledge-building unit distinct from the mind. According to the author, "we are constantly learning and teaching and we don't realise this process. The central issue is that if we don't realise it, we inevitably don't consider this process and the knowledge generated from it in our teaching practice" (CIAVATTA, 2009, p. 25). In my teaching activity, I began to consider the body as a unit for constructing knowledge only after getting to know the O Passo method, and today I realise how effective this awareness is for my students' understanding and rhythmic development.

b) Representation

According to Ciavatta (2009), the attitude of closing one's eyes to play, sing or listen to a piece of music - quite common among musicians in general - significantly alters and defines the way in which this activity takes place. According to the author,

> With our eyes closed, if we have learnt the music from a score, we can still see it. And at the same time, in an often indistinct whole, we will see the piano keyboard and our hands playing it. We'll see the friend who taught us music. Perhaps the house mentioned in the song's title? And even a blue background that moves incessantly. All these mental representations serve as references and help us when making music. Some of them we construct from concrete objects or real actions, which we somehow relate to that piece of music, such as the score, the instrument, the teacher; and some of them, abstract, entirely subjective, we compose from the most varied stimuli, such as a colour, a movement or a sensation (CIAVATTA, 2009, p. 28).

Bruner (apud CIAVATTA, 2009), when dealing with the "ways of elaborating and representing information on the environment", classifies these ways as follows:

1. Active - through action and manipulation;
2. Iconic - through perceptual organisation and auditory, kinaesthetic and visual imagery;

3. Symbolic - through words and other symbols.

According to Ciavatta, these representations are images that, in addition to forming structures whose elements are inseparable from each other, involve movement in their complexity, because, according to theorists reviewed by the author of the method, when visual images are present during an appreciation, they are always images of movement.

Thus, the representation of a rhythm is expressed in every part of the body of the person making music. According to the author, the body that makes music affects the mental representation of that making and, at the same time, the mental representation of that making affects the body that endeavours to make it. Ciavatta illustrates this by quoting Dalcroze (apud CIAVATTA, 2009)

> When a student makes a rhythm mistake on the piano, their teacher's limbs involuntarily try to correct it, not just by beating time (this is a conscious gesture, with a definite pedagogical purpose), but by a spontaneous effort of the whole body to put the accent in the right place. Not just one of his limbs, but <u>all his limbs contract simultaneously, introducing energy into his muscles and transmitting to the student the image of what he himself should have felt when he made the mistake</u>. For he himself must have been guided by the representation of the rhythm, reflected in all the muscles of his body (DALCROZE apud CIAVATTA, 2009, p. 29, my emphasis).

Considering the above quote, Ciavatta states that, in music teaching, various types of knowledge, other than those involving symbolic representation, should be considered as fundamental, such as, for example, in addition to the score and theoretical concepts, body movement in the representation of rhythm.

c) Group

Ciavatta (2009) says that making music together presupposes listening simultaneously to the sound produced by oneself and the sound produced by others, and that there are differences in attitudes towards listening only to oneself or to oneself and someone else, but that there is no difference in the number of "others", so whether in a practice between the individual plus one other, or twenty others, the attitude is the same:

> As long as we are unfamiliar with the sound we produce, our control over our listening will be precarious. We will either observe isolation, where we will only hear ourselves and there will be no interaction that makes joint practice effective, or dispersion, where we will only hear the sound of the other, and, not being able to control our own sound, joint practice will likewise be made impossible (CIAVATTA, 2009, p. 34).

That's why, in the O Passo method, interaction is achieved almost exclusively through polyphonic realisation. Comparing the unison approach with polyphonic realisation, the author states that in a unison practice, when the individual "gets it wrong", they have precise references that can make them "get it right" again. However, the author warns that the problem lies in the fact that this process may not involve awareness, because often the student doesn't know exactly where or how they went wrong, and if they get it right again, they don't know exactly how it happened. "In unison, the same dynamic that supports them also prevents them from understanding their mistakes and successes, protects them from their ignorance and leads them to remain in it" (Ciavatta, 2009, p. 36). The author concludes that only in polyphonic practice is the individual challenged to review the references they have built up and, through dialogue, to create new references and share their music-making collectively.

d) Culture

Regarding culture, considering the breadth of the concept, the author says he is specifically interested in "understanding how a culture operates on and is operated by the individuals who make it" (p. 36). Ciavatta (2009) observes that, unconsciously, in every word, every act, every gesture, there is a movement by the individual to define and be defined by a culture. The author cites Mauss (apud CIAVATTA, 2009), in his work entitled "Body Techniques", on body movements, in which he states that each small gesture translates elements of a given society or culture.

Lafraia (apud Ciavatta, 2009) explains that:

> Man is the result of the cultural environment in which he has been socialised. He is the heir to a long process of accumulation, which reflects the knowledge and experience acquired by the many generations that preceded him. The appropriate and creative manipulation of this cultural heritage allows for innovations and inventions. These are therefore not the product of the isolated action of a genius, but the result of the efforts of an entire community (p. 37).

Ciavatta (2009) states that the idea that seems most important is that all the elements that concern culture are involved in dynamic processes, because "there is no sense, or even the possibility, of establishing paralysing dualisms of the type individual versus culture, or new versus old, or erudite culture versus popular culture. There is only dialogue, interaction" (p. 37). Considering the principles and pillars of the O Passo method, which are its ideological foundations, the concepts and tools of O Passo are presented below.

3.3 Concepts and tools of the Step method

Reflecting on his method, the author mentions that:

> O Passo introduced new concepts into the teaching and learning of rhythm and sound, such as position and musical space, and new tools, such as the gait that gives the method its name, oral notations and and the Partitura d'O Passo (CIAVATTA, 2009, p. 15).

The relevance of these concepts and tools for music education seems obvious to me, but despite the fact that there may be similarities with other methods, I believe that the systematisation of these elements is what sets the O Passo method apart.

Thus, the concept of musical space, according to Ciavatta (2004', is used in response to a supposed property of sound, proposed by the theorists reviewed in his dissertation. In addition to duration, timbre, intensity and pitch, the concept of musical movement can be found in the bibliography. One of these theorists, Thurmond (apud CIAVATTA, 2004) defines movement as follows:

> In psychology, musical rhythm depends on the fact that tones presented in a temporal sequence are perceived as having not only pitch, intensity, timbre, and duration, but also movement. Movement is exactly the progression from one note to another in a melody, so the term is a literal use of the word (THURMOND apud CIAVATTA, 2004, p. 36).

However, Lucas Ciavatta warns that although this movement can be taken literally, it differs from real movements because it doesn't take place in a real, concrete space. This movement, according to the author, takes place in a represented space, "a musical space, an interval of time that takes on a form when it is represented from a musical performance" (CIAVATTA, 2009, p. 37).

The concept of position, according to the author, arises to localise events within this musical space and "is what will allow us to say where this event comes from and where it goes, to understand its musical movement" (ibidem, p.38). This concept is, according to the author, the 5th property of sound. The author also uses this concept as a response to the Greek terms arsis (upbeat, suspension) and thesis (downbeat, rest).

According to the author, arsis and thesis are terms that name the differences between specific areas of musical space, and that these areas cause events (sounds or pauses) to move, for example, from a "weak" area to a "strong" area. Ciavatta states that the terms can be associated with denominations such as "weak and strong", "of suspension and rest", or even "high and low" (suggesting a relief for time, approximating the Greek suggestion of defining thesis through walking).[4]

He adds that

> Although the definition of what is meant by "weak time" and "strong time" can be raised as an issue, the important thing is that the concepts of arsis and thesis were not born to express accent pure and simple. Their origins are mainly linked to the Greeks' need to deal with a difference; a musical difference, subjective but real. Playing a note in time is undeniably easier than playing the same note in time signature (CIAVATTA, 2009, p. 46,).

In this way, he argues that the main intention of the concept of position is to map trajectories and contribute to the perception of the musical movements involved, and that this "mapping", according to the ideology of the method, should take place through body movement.

It can be seen that Lucas Ciavatta corroborates the authors reviewed so far in relation to the use of body movements for the purposes of music education. According to the author, body movements are one of

[4] According to Thurmond (apud CIAVATTA, 1996, p. 37), in the relationship between rhythm and walking, arsis is the moment when the foot is lifted to take a step (weak tempo), and thesis is the moment when the foot is on the ground (strong tempo).

the forms of musical notation. Ciavatta (2009) states that every musician uses some kind of musical notation, which can be categorised as: oral, bodily and graphic[5] . Below are some examples of these types of notation:

1) Oral: guitarists when verbally referring to notes/chords on the instrument such as "Iª house and 3ª string"; when verbally using note and chord names such as "mi, do, ré", in short, any musical information communicated verbally;
2) Bodily: conductors use body movement patterns to communicate musical information; instrumentalists when demonstrating notes/chords on the instrument ("this one, then this one");
3) Graphics: traditional score, harmonic maps, chord diagrams, etc.

In The Step method, specific notations are proposed for each type mentioned above and, related to this, other specific characteristics of the method are:

1) Work systematically and simultaneously with oral, body and graphic notation;
2) Using vowels and numbers in their graphic notation, so in O Passo, "knowing how to speak" (oral notation) a rhythm necessarily means "knowing how to write it" (graphic notation);
3) Working systematically with body notation.

Therefore, in O Passo, "walking" is a specific form of conducting with the feet, which, together with flexing the legs, stretching the legs, and clapping (grave and acute), form the basis of the method's body notations. Regarding the relationship between body notation and oral and graphic notation, Ciavatta states that,

> The body notation of O Passo, which arises from the establishment of a direct relationship between each of the moments of body movement and each of the tempos and their divisions, draws a "map", constructs at the level of representation a space to localise musical events, a musical space. Each of these places occupied by each of the events is given a name through oral notation: the times of a bar are associated with "numbers" (which depend on the number of times per bar) and the moments when the feet touch the ground. In simple division: time signatures are associated with "e"s (pronounced "ês") and the moments when the legs are flexed; divisions in four are associated with "i"s and the moments between flexing and extending the legs. In the compound division: the divisions in three to "o"s (pronounced: ôs) and the divisions in six to "i"s (CIAVATTA, 2009, p. 78).

Still on this subject, according to the author, "because it uses vowels and numbers in its graphic notation, in O Passo, 'knowing how to speak' a rhythm necessarily means 'knowing how to write it'" (ibid., p. 77), which brings us to the Partitura d'O Passo. Regarding the O Passo score, Ciavatta (2009) states that it basically has the same structure as the traditional score, but that its main aim is to introduce decoding processes

[5] According to Persellin (1992), music education researchers agree that musical memory can involve one or more modalities: visual, auditory and kinaesthetic, and that individuals have different preferences and learning styles based on these modalities.

for the latter, which is intended to reduce the difficulty level of the task of reading it. By means of numbers and vowels, O Passo's score graphically expresses bodily sensations - present in bodily notations - associated with musical ideas - which is reminiscent of strategy number 2 "Writing counts in the score", indicated by Lehmann and McArthur (2002), reviewed earlier. Comparing the two types of score, Ciavatta observes that

> The traditional score uses graphic spaces (the distance between one symbol and another) to represent time spaces; O Passo's score uses graphic spaces to represent musical spaces, already previously defined by O Passo's body notation (CIAVATTA, 2009, p. 79).

In order to highlight the concept of "musical space", the author exemplifies some bars written with the rhythmic notation of the O Passo score. Below (see Figure 1 - Score Comparison) is a comparison of what these bars, according to Ciavatta, could represent in the traditional score.

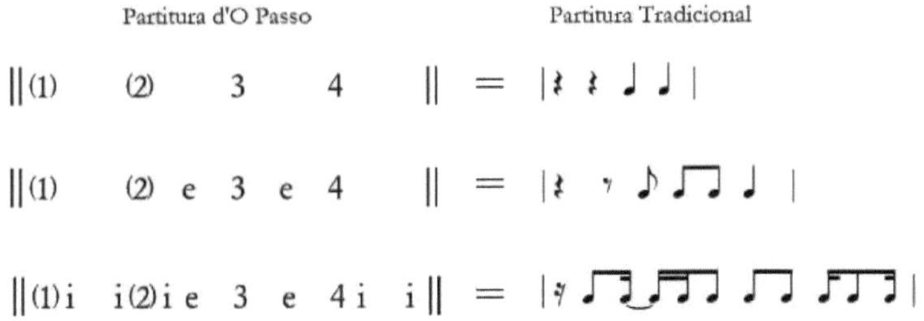

FIG. 1 - COMPARISON OF PARTITURES

You can see in figure 1 that, in the traditional score, the graphic space occupied by the bars varies according to need, which is imposed by the quantity and quality of elements. This is not the case in O Passo's score, since its principle is to represent musical spaces, which in practice means that, for example, a 4-stroke bar will always occupy the same space, both graphically and musically, regardless of the number of elements, divisions, present in it. Another characteristic is that all the bars and elements in it are perfectly aligned, as they are always in the same positions. Here again we are reminded of the similarity with strategy number 3 "Draw vertical lines, which indicate the alignment of the notes", highlighted by Lehmann and McArthur (2002), reviewed earlier.

As with the increasing order of complexity of the bars in the figure above, the method has rhythmic exercise sheets following the same logic. For this research, we used the number sheet, which generally corresponds to the quarter notes and their rests, and the "e" sheet (which divides the pulse into 2) and generally corresponds to the eighth note division and its respective rests (See APPENDIX I - Number Sheet and APPENDIX II - "e" Sheet).

In the score of O Passo, in relation to the representation of the duration parameter, the author considers that this

> [...] it can't, and doesn't pretend to, deal with the question of note durations, but rather indicates their positions. However, when it comes to learning durations, practice has shown me that knowing the positions is as useful for knowing when to start a sound as it is for knowing when to stop it. Which, in practice, means solving the question of durations (CIAVATTA, 2009, p. 79).

The use of syllables, letters and words as a tool for learning rhythm is a resource used by different music education methods. Considering comparisons between different approaches and the O Passo method, here is Colley's research (1988), in which the author analyses and compares methods that use syllables, letters and words as tools for learning rhythm. The following image (see Figure 2 - Comparisons of syllabic methods) shows examples of different methodologies and their relationship with traditional score writing.

FIG. 2 - COMPARISONS OF SILAR METHODS (SOURCE: COLLEY, 1982)

Colley's research (1982) found that the participants seemed to understand rhythms more easily when they were subjected to methods that used specific words to understand different rhythmic cells, compared to those that only used letters, syllables and/or numbers. In this sense, Ciavatta warns that

> [...] the absence of body notation associated with other forms of oral notation, different from the form used in O Passo, is what explains its limitations as a tool for building knowledge. Someone who says, for example, "CHO-CO-LA-TE" to try to understand the four-part division of the pulse doesn't necessarily understand, localise or master each of the divisions. This person would not be able, simply by speaking the whole word in a musical context, to speak only one of the syllables while keeping it in this context. (CIAVATTA, 2009, p. 77).

Frank Abrahams (2010), who is a professor at Westminster Choir College of Rider University in Princeton, USA, and also the author of the chapter "O *Passo (The Step), a Critical Pedagogy for Music*

Education from Brazil', which is part of the book '*Alternative Approaches to Music Education*', defines O Passo as a Brazilian critical pedagogy that provides students with tools that empower them to be musicians. Abrahams (2010) also states that the method bridges the gap between what students hear/like and the musical content normally covered in music lessons. The researcher also considers that the method is a "catalyst" for the individual's musical autonomy, and that teachers in the United States who use the method report enthusiasm on the part of the students and notice improvements in both their musical abilities and their attitudes towards music lessons. These points reflect aspects present in studies in the area of motivation, and this theme will be addressed in the next chapter.

CHAPTER 4

MOTIVATION FOR LEARNING MUSIC

Learning a skill such as music reading involves the student not only in cognitive processes, but also, as we will see here, psychological processes. Sloboda states that

> The feeling of a multitude of demands and the impossibility of meeting them all is a characteristic of the beginning of learning in any activity. This feeling can be highly discouraging, and can cause the learner to give up before any progress has been made (SLOBODA, 2008, p. 287).

Considering the complexity and requirements for the development of music reading, and the fact that, regardless of age or level of musical training, any individual can be a beginner in this activity, the above statement is also valid for the object of study of this research.

According to Araújo (2010), motivation is the fact that drives people's actions and choices, and is present in all types of human activity. In her chapter "Motivation and Music Teaching" (2010), the author reviews theorists from psychology, education and other areas that relate to motivation. On the concepts of this term, the author states that

> [...] for Bzuneck, the suggestive idea that applies to the term comes from the etymological root of the word itself, which comes from the Latin verb movere, which in turn originates the noun *motivum*, or "motive", in other words, motivation is an element that generates an action, which moves the individual to fulfil a specific function. For this author, therefore, motivation can be understood both as a psychological factor (or set of factors) and as a process, which helps and ensures that human beings persist and direct their attention and the development of the activities carried out (ARAÚJO, 2010, p. 111).

With regard to the relationship between motivation and learning, according to Bzuneck (2009) student motivation is perhaps the main determinant of the success and quality of learning because, according to the author, it is a complex and multifaceted variable that cannot be taught or trained as if it were a skill or knowledge. He also warns that motivation influences and is influenced by learning outcomes.

Araújo (2015) reviewing Guimarães and Bzuneck (apud ARAÚJO, 2015) in a reference to the school environment, motivation has been seen as an essential element for the level of performance and quality of learning, and that intrinsic motivation is the one that best represents the positive potential of human nature. According to Araújo (2010),

> The subject of motivation has been approached in music research through different approaches linked to various sub-areas such as cognition, performance practices, music education, with varied approaches such as motivation for musical learning, performance aspects and motivation, motivational theories and musical development, among others. (ARAÚJO, 2010, pp. 120-121)

It is therefore possible to deduce that motivation is highly significant in the process of learning music. Araújo (2015) states that motivation is fundamental for those who experience music and that it is an element that guarantees the quality of the individual's involvement in this process. He adds:

> From this cognitivist approach to motivation, we can understand that music practice, teaching and learning are activities driven by emotional, cognitive and subjective factors, as well as being influenced by situations and conditions in the social context. Teachers need motivation to teach music, and students need motivation to learn. In short, the musician needs to be motivated so that the results of their practice generate satisfaction and success. This motivation, in turn, can be intensified. These processes of intensifying motivation can be thought of in the light of different theories [...] (ARAÚJO, 2015, p. 47)

According to McPherson and O'Neill (2002), recent theories see motivation as an integral part of musical learning, and the aims of studies in this area are to understand how and why individuals learn:

- Develop a desire to study music;
- They value this learning;
- The degree of persistence and intensity in this study varies;
- Evaluate and attribute success and failure in different contexts.

Corroborating this statement, Araújo (2015) adds that "the study of motivation theories has provided researchers, teachers and musicians with the

the opportunity to get to know *the* psychological mechanisms that exist in the processes of the subject's involvement with music" (p. 48).

According to the author, one of the theories that can help teachers, musicians and students in this regard is the Self-Determination Theory, developed by Deci and Ryan between 1975 and 1991. These theorists, Araújo (2015) points out, when analysing and discussing intrinsic and extrinsic factors, point to different levels of extrinsic motivation, according to the self-determination continuum shown in figure 3:

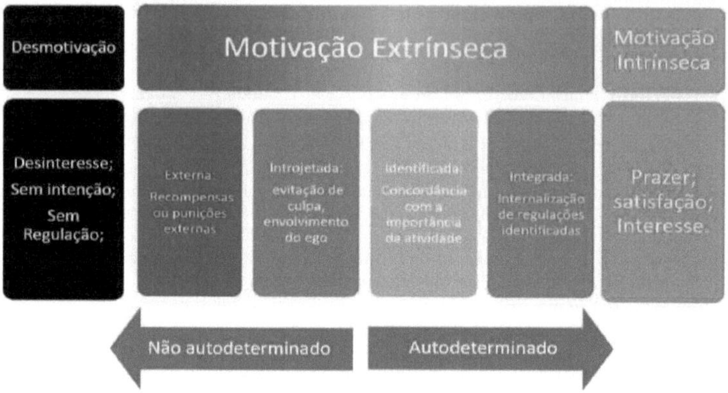

FIG. 3 - SELF-DETERMINATION CONTINUUM

According to Araújo (2015), depending on how the individual perceives and assimilates the internal factors that move them towards a particular action, they can qualitatively experience different types of extrinsic motivation regulation, which are divided into external, introjected, identified and integrated, the latter being qualitatively similar to intrinsic motivation.

The author states that extrinsic motivation, in this sense, contrary to common sense, is not a negative motivation, because the greater the level of internalisation of extrinsic factors by the individual, the greater their capacity for self-determination - in the figure above, the level of self-determination (or self-determined behaviour) is increasing from left to right, in relation to the types of extrinsic motivation regulations.

Considering the musical and educational environment, it is important to note that:

> In the process of musical practice/learning, this theory signals the importance of the role of the teacher, parents and peers, as well as social factors in this process. In other words, if the student/musician is encouraged/stimulated externally to study a certain repertoire [or skill, such as LPV], for example, he or she can reach a level of appropriation of these external elements through "identification" and appreciation of the action, becoming increasingly motivated. Many factors can contribute to this internalisation movement, such as incentives and appreciation of the action by other subjects (teachers, parents, colleagues); the student's own observation of the results of their study, which makes them feel confident about their abilities; involvement in the study process; and increasing personal appreciation of the results obtained, which generates greater autonomy in the individual to carry out different musical activities (ARAÚJO, 2015, p. 49).

In this way, the complexity of the aspects involved in the action is evident. Finally, Araújo also presents the analysis of self-efficacy beliefs, which, according to Bzuneck (apud ARAÚJO, 2015), consists of "the personal assessment or perception that the individual makes about their abilities, their intelligence, their knowledge, in short, their personal capacities and skills" (p. 50). According to Viera and Coimbra (apud ARAÚJO, 2015), "when the individual asks: 'Will I be able to do it?' they are asking themselves about their self-efficacy beliefs in relation to something" (id.).

Self-efficacy beliefs are the core of the Social Cognitive Theory, developed by Albert Bandura, which focuses on human motivational behaviour while inserted in a social context. Araújo (2015, p. 50) states that self-efficacy "indicates a level of motivation in which subjects act based on their convictions, therefore an affective-based motivation".

According to Bandura (apud ARAÚJO, 2015), this belief cannot be confused with self-esteem or the belief that "the results of certain activities are caused by external behaviours or 'forces'" (p. 50). These beliefs, according to Pajares and Olaz (apud ARAÚJO, 2015), are formed from different factors, such as personal experiences of success, vicarious experiences (observation), persuasive verbalisations and emotional reactions. Figure 4 shows the relationship between Self-Efficacy Beliefs and the factors that form them.

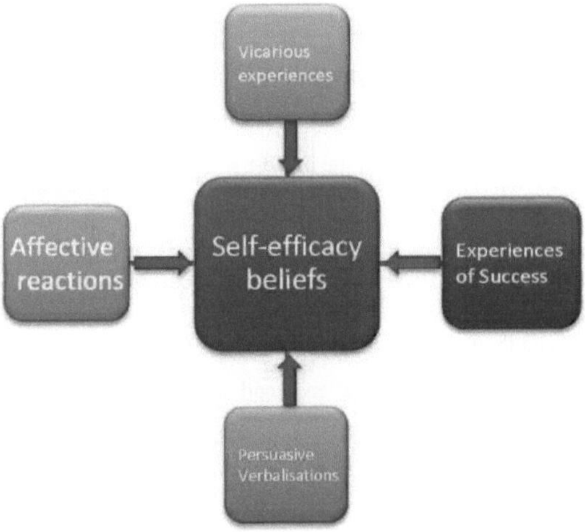

FIG. 4 - SELF-EFFECTIVE BELIEFS

According to these authors,

> Self-efficacy beliefs help determine how much effort people will put into an activity, how long they will persevere when faced with obstacles, and how resilient they will be in the face of adverse situations [...]. As a consequence, self-efficacy beliefs also influence the choices people make and the courses of action they pursue. Individuals tend to select tasks and activities that make them feel competent (PAJAREZ AND OLAZ apud ARAÚJO, 2015, p. 51).

Below is a schematic figure that represents, according to the quote above, the influence of self-efficacy beliefs on individuals' behaviour (see Figure 5 - Influence of self-efficacy beliefs).

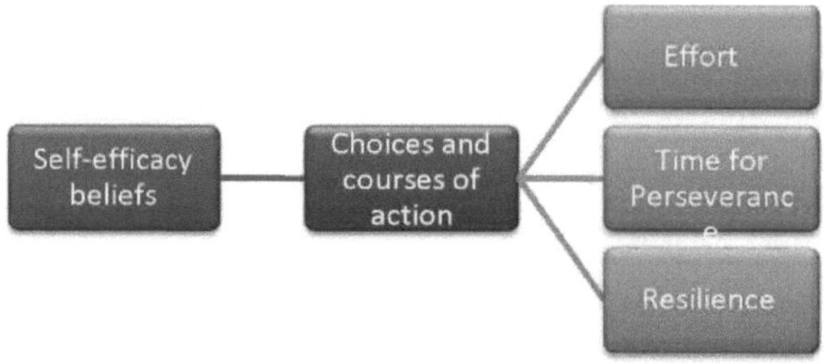

FIG. 5 - INFLUENCE OF SELF-EFFECTIVE BELIEFS

Araújo and Gonçalves (2014) carried out a study on self-efficacy beliefs for the subject of musical perception in a higher education context. The authors developed questionnaires with self-efficacy scales following Bandura's own guidelines. The results showed that the increase in self-efficacy beliefs is directly proportional to the time spent studying music, i.e. the greater the student's musical experience, the greater their self-efficacy beliefs for the subject's tasks. The results also showed that the highest self-efficacy beliefs were related to rhythmic activities, and the lowest to managing study outside the classroom environment.

Araújo (2015) then presents Csikszentmihalyi's Flow Theory. The author states that, according to Csikszentmihalyi, the experience of flow occurs when a certain task is performed by the subject in which there is a balance between the challenges they must face and their abilities to do so. This "state of flow" makes the individual who is concentrating on such an activity (which balances challenge and skill) lose track of time, feel joy/satisfaction and a sense of well-being. However, when there is no balance, other emotional states can arise, as shown in figure 6.

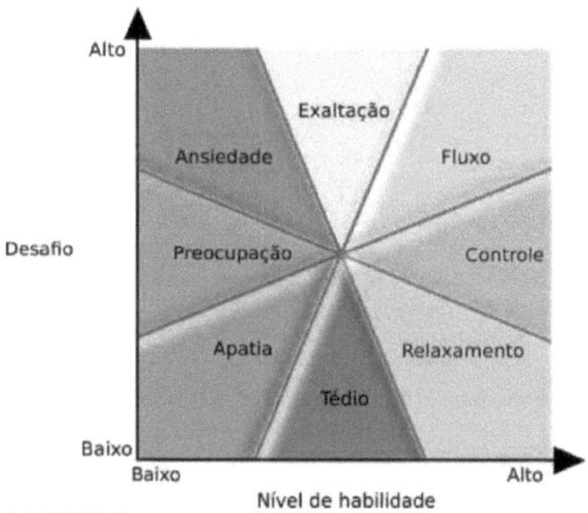

FIG. 6-FLOW

According to the graph, if the challenges are too high in relation to the level of ability, anxiety and worry will arise. On the other hand, if their skills and capacities are above the challenges, the individual will find the task very easy and will tend to relax, and may experience boredom and apathy.

According to Csikszentmihalyi (apud ARAÚJO, 2015), some factors can help the process of experiencing flow, such as goal setting, cognitive operation (concentration) and the experience of emotions. These factors are in a kind of order of occurrence and dependence, because:

> Focusing on goals helps them [the individual] to move on to a stage of concentration, that is, to a process of cognitive operation that focuses psychic energy and orders attention. Therefore, having clear goals and a focus of attention, you can experience flow, and this experience is emotionally charged, i.e. a positive emotion such as joy, happiness, satisfaction (ARAÚJO, 2015, p. 52).

Lessa (2015), in her dissertation, approaches the O Passo method from the perspective of Flow Theory in the context of a carnival block in Rio de Janeiro (Sargento Pimenta). According to her, the data collected was indicative of the experience of flow, because:

1) The participants were involved in the activities with dedication to studying the pages of O Passo;
2) The method's activities provided challenges for most of the participants, while also providing the basis for overcoming these challenges through their structuring, goals and clear feedback;
3) High levels of concentration were observed during the block rehearsals and for the experience of losing track of time, experienced by the vast majority of participants and which is also indicative of the experience of flow.

For Lessa, the Step method has a gradual complexity to ensure that you acquire the basic skills you need and then move on to more complex ones, which guarantees a balance between challenges and skills.

Bearing in mind the aspects pointed out in this chapter, the use of the O Passo method for learning and developing rhythmic sight-reading can be considered in the light of motivation studies, taking into account the contribution that this approach can make to analysing and understanding the process of developing this skill.

CHAPTER 5

METHODOLOGY

Considering the objectives of this research, the methodology chosen as most appropriate was quasi-experimental research. According to Gil (2008), quasi-experimental is a type of research which, although it does not have random distribution of subjects or control groups, is very close to experimental, as it is developed with a great deal of methodological rigour. Therefore, the analysis of cause-effect relationships can be obtained by comparing treatment and non-treatment conditions with the same subjects before treatment (GIL, 2008).

Thus, the first stage of this research consisted of surveying subjects who could be possible participants in the research. This stage took place through direct contact with students on a music teacher training course for basic education. The criteria for selecting effective participants were as follows:

- Being a student on a second degree music course in the city of Curitiba-PR;
- Working as a teacher in music education;
- No knowledge or experience of the O Passo method or the O Passo score;
- Volunteer to take part in the research.

The procedures for carrying out the research were:

- Preparation and application of the pre-test and initial questionnaire;
- Application of activities with the method;
- Preparation and application of the post-test and final questionnaire.

Before the pre-test and the start of the activities with the method, the participants signed the term of participation and consent to the research procedures (see APPENDIX), and answered the initial questionnaire (see APPENDIX IV - Initial Questionnaire).

The questionnaire contained questions designed to characterise the participant in terms of age, gender, length of time studying music and, from the participant's point of view, their level of music reading (rhythm and pitch) and what they thought about music reading.

The pre-test (see ANNEX V - Pre-test) consisted of a video recording of the participants' individual performance (in isolation from the others) as they performed, if they so chose, 3 rhythm sheets of increasing difficulty (with 4 bars each, using the 4/4 formula, including quarter notes, eighth notes and their respective breaks). With 3 sheets, each with 4 bars, there are 12 possible bars per participant. Therefore, multiplying this value by the total number of participants gives the group 120 bars for the pre-test.

It was to be carried out after the participant had briefly looked at the sheet in question and, if they chose, they would start reading it at first glance (without rehearsal, without the possibility of correction and without stopping). There was no timer for the activity.

The criteria for evaluating these videotaped performances were established at a meeting with my supervisor. We therefore decided to use 1 bar as the unit of measurement for this assessment. Therefore, the participant had to perform all the elements of that bar correctly for it to be considered a hit. I evaluated the videos and transcribed the data obtained from this material individually.

The activities using the method were carried out by the Percussion teacher on the course, and there was no interference from me (the researcher) in this process. The teacher had knowledge of and experience with the O Passo method prior to these activities. After practising the method and before starting the post-test, the participants answered a final questionnaire (See ANNEX V - Final Questionnaire), which contained questions designed to investigate the individual's experience with the O Passo method.

The post-test (see ANNEX VI - Post-Test) consisted of the same procedure as the pre-test, with 3 rhythm sheets of increasing difficulty, with 4 bars of 4/4 time on each sheet, including quarter notes, eighth notes and their respective rests. With 3 sheets, each with 4 bars, there are 12 possible bars per participant. Therefore, multiplying this value by the total number of participants gives the group, as in the pre-test, 120 bars for the post-test.

As in the pre-test, the participant had to make a brief observation of the sheet in question and, if he or she chose, start reading the sheet at first glance (without rehearsal, without the possibility of correction and without stopping). However, because the object of the research was rhythmic reading at first sight, different sheets from the previous ones were prepared for this occasion, considering that the level of difficulty should be the same. The following chapters will present the data and analyse it in the light of the bibliography reviewed in this dissertation.

5.1 Data presentation and analysis

The participants were selected from a percussion class on a course to train music teachers for basic education at a public higher education institution in the city of Curitiba-PR. The participants had no prior knowledge of the O Passo method. Of the 12 students, 10 answered the initial questionnaire, 10 took part in the pre-test and post-test, and 12 answered the final questionnaire. Firstly, the data relating to the initial questionnaire will be presented (See ANNEX IV - Initial Questionnaire).

The timetable for the course, previously planned by the teacher in charge, already envisaged working with the O Passo method as the basis for developing the activities. However, considering the objectives of the research, the teacher in charge added exercises focussing on the O Passo score and its correspondence with the traditional score to the lesson plans for the period of the experiment.

Initial Questionnaire

The first information required in the questionnaire was the age and gender of the participants. All the participants were women aged between 33 and 50.

The first question asked how long the participant had been studying music and indicated that, of the 10 participants who answered the initial questionnaire, 8 had been studying music for 3 years, 1 for 4 years and another for 6 years.The second question asked if the participant played an instrument and which instrument(s). The answers are shown below:

Instrument	Number of participants playing
Flute	6
Keyboard	1
Guitar	4
Piano	2
Organ	1
None	1

TAB. 1 - INSTRUMENTS

Question number 3, a single-choice objective question, asked whether the participant knew how to read notes and/or rhythms. The answer options were "yes", "no" or "more or less". The following graph shows the answers (see Figure 7 - Knowledge of Music Reading).

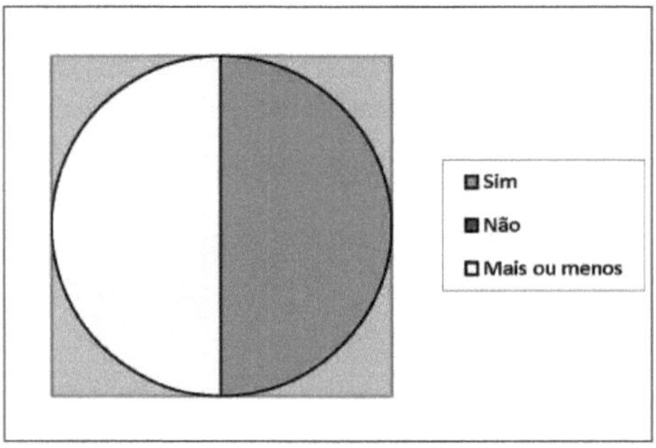

FIG. 7 - KNOWLEDGE OF MUSICAL READING

All the participants said they had at least some knowledge of music reading. According to Marino and Ramos (2003), reading and writing music are essential for musical mastery and understanding, and so these individuals fulfil this requirement, at least in part. According to Ciavatta (2009) and Boyle (1970), music reading promotes the individual's musical autonomy, remedying limitations, and therefore the participants have some level of this autonomy.

Question 4, a single-choice objective, was related to the previous question and asked the participant, if they had answered "yes" or "more or less", to tick the skill they were referring to in their answer, whether it was reading rhythms and/or pitches. The following table shows this data (see Table 2 - Music Reading Skills).

Skills	Number of participants
Rhythm Reading	1
Height reading	4
Both	5

TAB. 2 - MUSICAL READING SKILLS

Of the 10 participants, 9 said they had mastered pitch reading and 6 had mastered rhythm reading. Considering the fact that, although in many instruments the production of pitches is possible without the need to internalise these pitches, and that rhythmic reading requires auditory coding (SHEHAN, 1987), this data indicates that the majority of participants only mastered the part of the reading that does not require auditory coding.

Another issue that this data may suggest is that rhythmic reading skills are the main predictor of performance in a sight-reading task (BOYLE, 1970; ELLIOT, 1982; BEBEAU, 1982; HODGES, 1992; SHEHAN, 1987; MCPHERSON, 1994), i.e. the 40 per cent (4 participants) who said they only mastered pitch reading may not perform well in a sight-reading task as well as in a rhythmic sight-reading task (the primary objective of this research).

Question 5, which was divided into two parts, the first part being a single-choice objective and the second an open-ended discursive question, asked the participant if they thought learning to read was relevant to musical practice, and then asked them to justify their answer. All the participants answered "yes", in other words, they all said that they considered learning to read music to be relevant to their practice.

The justifications given by the participants were as follows:

> Reading sheet music is important if you want to start learning an instrument.
>
> Reading sheet music is fundamental for musicians who play an instrument and also for choral singers, classical singers and even MPB singers.
>
> It's important for the teacher to know how to read in order to be able to teach and understand the music. I don't think it's necessary for students (mainstream education), only for students who go outside of school.
>
> In terms of knowledge, a foundation for teaching music in schools. In terms of practising instruments, it is much more relevant for deepening practice and performance as an instrumentalist.
>
> As a teacher, I think so, as a form of knowledge to develop what the SIME music curriculum asks for[6] .
>
> The performance of the music itself will be more complete with score reading.
>
> By knowing how to read sheet music, there is greater access to repertoires.
>
> Especially as a teacher, it is essential to know first in order to teach.

[6] SIME - I couldn't find any reference to this acronym. Perhaps the participant was mistaken in her intention to write SME, which stands for Municipal Education Secretariat.

Reading is extremely necessary. To be able to teach, you need to know.

It's another access to the repertoire.

It can be seen from the responses that the participants perceive the importance and necessity of reading music, whether for learning an instrument or singing, for teacher training, curriculum fulfilment, access to repertoires, etc. These data indicate, according to Self-Determination Theory (DECI and RYAN apud ARAÚJO, 2015), that the participants have extrinsic motivations for reading music, and that these differ qualitatively by their regulations, which can be classified as external - obtaining a reward or avoiding punishment (reward for becoming a teacher, fulfilling a curriculum, etc.), and identified - agreement with the importance of the activity (access to repertoire, for the teacher to understand and teach music, etc.).

One participant said that she didn't think learning to read music was relevant for students in mainstream education, only for those who sought it outside of school, which, according to the theorists reviewed so far, would limit the individual's experiences and autonomy.

In the following sections, the pre-test and post-test stages are presented and analysed in the light of the literature review, with their respective data, as well as the data from the final questionnaire.

Pre-test

In this section, the data relating to the participants' performance in the pre-test will be presented in tabular form (see Table 3 - Pre-Test Evaluation). The data is the result of an evaluation that took into account the participant's execution when reading the pre-test sheets at first glance, the number of hits and errors they made when executing each bar. To indicate the data, an "OK" was used for the right bars, an "X" for the wrong bars, and the abbreviation NE for the bars not played.

The instructions given to the participants were as follows:

1) The participant could briefly look at the sheet in question and choose whether or not to perform it;
2) If they chose to do it, they had to read it continuously;
3) The tempo had to be set by the participant themselves, who had to keep it up until the end of the sheet in question;
4) The use of any form of regency, whether traditional or with foot markings, for example, was permitted;
5) The execution could be with claps or other forms of body percussion or even with a phoneme, but the pitch would not be assessed;
6) When they finished one sheet, they had to do the same with the next one (if there was

one).

The results obtained from all the participants have therefore been grouped together and summarised in the following table:

Pre-test	Sheet 1				Sheet 2				Sheet 3			
Participant	CI	C2	C3	C4	CI	C2	C3	C4	CI	C2	C3	C4
pre.1	X	X	X	X	**OK**	**OK**	**OK**	**OK**	**OK**	X	X	X
pre.2	**OK**	**OK**	**OK**	**OK**	X	X	X	X	X	X	X	X
pre.3	**OK**	**OK**	**OK**	**OK**	X	X	X	X	X	X	X	X
pre.4	**OK**	**OK**	**OK**	**OK**	X	**OK**	**OK**	**OK**	**OK**	X	X	X
pre.5	**OK**	**OK**	**OK**	**OK**	X	X	X	X	X	X	X	X
pre.6	X	X	X	X	X	X	X	X	NE	NE	NE	NE
pre.7	**OK**	**OK**	**OK**	**OK**	X	X	X	X	NE	NE	NE	NE
pre.8	**OK**	X	**OK**	**OK**	X	X	X	X	NE	NE	NE	NE
pre.9	**OK**	**OK**	**OK**	**OK**	**OK**	**OK**	**OK**	X	**OK**	X	X	X
pre.10	**OK**	**OK**	**OK**	**OK**	X	**OK**	**OK**	**OK**	**OK**	X	X	X

TAB. 3 - PRE-TEST EVALUATION

Based on the table above, the data on the participants' performance was as follows (see Table 4 - Pre-test hit margins):

Pre-test	HITS	MARGIN
SHEET 1	31/40	77,5%
SHEET 2	13/40	32,5%
SHEET 3	4/40	10%
TOTAL	**48/120**	**40%**

TAB. 4 - PRE-TEST ACCURACY MARGINS

The tables above show that the participants' best performance in the pre-test (see Appendix V - Pre-Test) was on Sheet 1 (77.5% correct), which only contains quarter notes and their respective rests. On Sheet 2, which contains quarter notes and eighth notes (but no eighth note breaks), performance fell to 32.5 per cent and on Sheet 3, which includes eighth note breaks, the margin of accuracy fell to 10 per cent.

The fact that the participants' performance was inversely proportional to the increase in difficulty of the tasks, and the marked difference between their performance on the different sheets are indications that, according to the flow theory (CSIKSZENTMIHALYI apud ARAÚJO, 2015), the level of difficulty of the tasks, at least on Sheets 2 and 3, was not balanced with the level of skill the participants had to carry them out.

This difficulty, which explains the low performance when including eighth notes and subsequently their rests, can be associated with the fact that, according to Ciavatta (2009), simply playing in time is undeniably easier than playing in time signature, and that familiarity with the codes contained in Sheet 2 (quarter notes, and eighth notes) and Sheet 3 (quarter notes, quarter note rests, eighth notes and eighth note rests) was considerably less familiar than the codes on Sheet 1 (quarter notes and quarter note rests), as the difference in complexity is evident.

This decrease in performance, according to Bebeau (1983), may also be associated with the fact that rhythmic reading is a difficult skill to acquire, and the participants' experience of reading music may have been through traditional methods that require the acquisition of mathematical concepts before they can be used, demanding concentration and a considerable amount of cognitive processing. In this way, as Bebeau warns, the participants in this research may have been tempted to merely approximate the duration value represented in the symbols.

Activities with the method

Immediately after the pre-test, the participants began the activities with the O Passo method, which were carried out in 6 lessons, 2 weekly lessons of 4 hours each. The lessons were based on the concepts and tools of the O Passo method, and during the 6 lessons the teacher dealt in particular with the oral and bodily notations corresponding to the graphic notation on the "Numbers (tempo)" sheet (see APPENDIX I - Numbers (tempo)) and on the "e (countertempo)" sheet (see APPENDIX II - e (countertempo)) of the O Passo score, also addressing its correspondence with the traditional score (see APPENDIX III - Correspondence between scores/Activities with the method).

After the classes with the activities using the method, the students answered the final questionnaire and then took the post-test. Firstly, the data from the final questionnaire will be presented.

Final Questionnaire

All 12 students answered the final questionnaire (see ANNEX VII - Final Questionnaire). For the sake of preserving the identity of those involved, no means have been found to identify the answers of the 2 participants who were not part of the experiment. The first question in this questionnaire was open-ended/discursive, and asked the participant about her experience with the O Passo method during the course, and asked her to point out aspects of this experience considering the concepts and tools of the method. The answers were as follows:

> It was excellent! I loved the method and I will certainly apply it in my teaching practice.
>
> I really enjoyed learning the O Passo method, because I thought it was great to use with students so that they could easily learn rhythmic notation, notation and time signature.
>
> It was a new experience, I didn't know this method, I thought it was very good to insert body movement into the reading of musical notes. It's easier to understand and realise musical reading than other formal methods.
>
> I think the class with the O Passo method should be at the beginning, because marking the rhythm in this method is much easier, we had a rhythm class [previously] and it was very difficult, with this method it would be easier.
>
> I really liked it because it helped me a lot with rhythmic reading, pulse and time signature. I think that if it had been introduced earlier it would have helped me a lot more.
>
> I didn't know it yet, I was curious and it cleared up a lot of doubts I had about rhythm. The counting/talking floor was a tool that helped a lot.

> It was very rewarding and important. With O Passo I was able to understand rhythmic readings better.
>
> My experience with the method has been enriching. I see it as valid for working with students in both the theoretical and practical aspects, for a better appropriation and understanding of the musical concepts directly involved in the process of developing the method.
>
> The method helps in the process of learning rhythmic figures, bars and pulse. It becomes easier to understand the score.
>
> The experience was very worthwhile since we had already studied the rhythmic part with another method that wasn't as effective as this one.
>
> It helped to resolve some initial difficulties with rhythm. However, I have a lot of difficulty with motor coordination, and I need more time to dedicate to studying.
>
> I had my first contact with the teacher [of this subject] and all the lessons required a lot of synchronisation and concentration. The experience was innovative in a common classroom environment. I found the score [of O Passo] very interesting and very different from what we're used to musically.

Considering the answers above, the aspects pointed out by the participants include:

1) Simple and effective learning of rhythm, its concepts and graphic writing (of the traditional score and the Partitura d'O Passo), especially in relation to the methods previously used by them.
2) Positive experience with body and oral notation of rhythm and its spelling.
3) Innovation for music education and the school environment (as opposed to traditional methods).

The participants' experience with the O Passo method for learning rhythm and rhythmic reading was positive, and the method was a motivating element in this process. This can be explained by the Flow Theory, because considering the results of the pre-test, there were clear and focussed goals in the preparation of the activities with the method, and the level of difficulty of the tasks was adapted to the level of skill displayed by the participants, which helped them to move on to a stage of concentration. From the answers, it can also be deduced that the participants possibly experienced flow, as the emotional charge indicated joy, happiness and satisfaction.

These results are consistent with those of Lessa's research (2015), in which it was observed that: 1) participants showed engagement with the method's activities due to: 1) the presence of gradual complexity in the tasks, 2) the means for overcoming challenges (structuring, goals and clear feedback) and; 3) because they showed high levels of concentration.

The participants' answers also include aspects that, according to the Social Cognitive Theory, are indicators of self-efficacy beliefs. According to this theory, the participants had personal experiences of success, i.e. they were able to carry out tasks; verbal persuasions such as positive influences from the teacher; vicarious experiences (observation), because as the lessons were in a group, they observed their colleagues, learnt and motivated themselves in this way. With clear goals about what to learn, about rhythm and rhythmic reading and the tools and concepts of the O Passo method, the participants thought they were capable of carrying out the tasks and were motivated to the point of saying that they would use them in their teaching activities.

It should also be noted that one of the participants reported difficulties with motor coordination, admitting that she would need more time to dedicate to her studies. According to Ciavatta (2009), this can be explained by the fact that this individual did not integrate the notions of space and time in order to organise their sensory system. By saying that she has difficulty with motor coordination, the participant may have revealed that she was deprived of bodily experiences and, according to the author, may not have built up the correct notions of space and time at her level of representation.

The second question, which was a single-choice objective, asked whether the participant considered the possibility of the O Passo method as a tool for learning rhythmic reading. The answer options were "yes", "no" or "I don't know". All the participants answered "yes". Considering the strategies for developing rhythmic reading given by Lehmann and McArthur (2002), the table below makes a comparison with the strategies and tools of the O Passo method (see Table 4 - Comparison of Strategies).

Lehmann and McArthur	**The Step (Ciavatta)**
Playing the rhythm by clapping (or with other forms of rhythmic body movements)	The body is one of the foundations of the method, and among the body notations, conducting with the feet is the rhythmic body movement that gives the method its name; clapping is also a type of body notation
Writing counts in the score	Through numbers and vowels, O Passo's score graphically expresses bodily sensations - present in body notations - associated with musical ideas
Draw vertical lines, which indicate the alignment of the notes	The score of 0 Passo uses graphic spaces to represent musical spaces that have already been defined by the body notation of O Passo, so all the bars and elements that are in them are perfectly aligned, as they are always in the same positions
Practise reading with the help of a metronome or a device with MIDI playback, such as a sequencer.	Not used
Playing in an accompaniment or ensemble practice situation with real performers	**0 group is one of the pillars of 0 Step**

TAB. 5 - COMPARISON OF STRATEGIES

The table above shows that the O Passo method fulfils practically all of Lehmann and McArthur's (2002) strategy indications, except for the use of a metronome or MIDI playback device. This fact is justified by Ciavatta (2009) when he says that O Passo uses a pulsating tempo, different from that measured by a metronome, and adds that

> Even if the execution of a pulsating tempo is subject to being considered right or wrong, we must not lose sight of the fact that we human beings produce absolutely normal variations and inaccuracies and cannot or should not be compared to machines.

> Machines don't "sweat" (p. 63).

The third question, also a single-choice objective question, asked whether the participant felt more confident in performing rhythmic reading after using the O Passo method. The answer options were "yes", "no" or "I don't know". All the participants answered "yes", and this corroborates the motivational aspects pointed out earlier when analysing the answers to question 1, in particular the association between the use of the O Passo Method and the development of self-efficacy beliefs (BANDURA, 2008).

The fourth question was made up of two parts, the first being a single-choice objective, and the second an open-ended question in which the participant had to justify their answer. The question was whether the participant would use activities from the Step method with her students in the classroom. The answer options for the first part were "yes", "no" or "I don't know". All the participants answered "yes". One participant did not justify her answer. The justifications of the others were as follows:

> Yes, I would, but in order to use it I'd have to have the domain first.
>
> The children certainly have rhythmic reading in their curriculum. Passo makes this reading much easier, because the child can experience the theoretical part with their body.
>
> I used it with the 2nd year of primary school, with the song "Drops de Hortelã" by Oswaldo Montenegro. They had no problems carrying out the practices proposed in the 1-2-3-4 scheme.
>
> I intend to use it in my next lessons involving rhythmic reading and practice.
>
> Because it's a very simple way of teaching rhythmic cells.
>
> Yes, because with this method they will learn rhythm in theory as well as in practice.
>
> I'm already using it and they like it very much.
>
> For rhythmic marking, which the students have a lot of difficulty with, it would be easier.
>
> It's easy to understand. I'd particularly like to do more courses on The Step.
>
> I didn't know the method and I was happy to learn about it before the end of the course. The activities are very dynamic and involve body expression, which I'm sure will be useful for working with my special education students.
>
> I would use it with secondary school pupils who already have musical experience and would possibly assimilate it more easily.

The responses show that the participants not only approve of the method, but have already used it or say they will use it in their teaching careers. Among the aspects highlighted are:

1) Facilitating the process of learning rhythm and rhythmic reading;
2) Learning rhythm in theory and practice;
3) The dynamism and bodily expressiveness of the activities enrich the experience.

This data also corroborates the analysis of self-efficacy beliefs, successful experiences and other factors that increase self-efficacy beliefs, which also make the individual have a self-efficacy belief for teaching. Bzuneck (2000) states that the influences of self-efficacy beliefs on behaviour and motivation in teachers can be summed up in four main items:

1) In setting goals for oneself: greater challenges are sought and faced by those with higher faced by those with higher self-efficacy beliefs;
2) The degree of effort the person will invest in the tasks: proportionally greater effort derives from stronger self-efficacy beliefs;
3) The degree of persistence, despite the difficulties along the way;
4) The way in which the person reacts to possible failures.

After answering the final questionnaire, the students took the post-test (See ANNEX VI - Post-Test), and the results are shown in the following section.

Post-test

In this section, data on the participants' performance in the post-test will be presented in tabular form (see Table 4 - Post-test evaluation). The procedure was identical to the pre-test. As before, the data is the result of an evaluation that takes into account the participant's execution when reading the post-test sheets at first glance (see ANNEX tal - Post-Test), the number of hits and errors she makes when executing each bar. The instructions given to the participants were similar to those used in the pre-test.[7]

Post-test	Sheet 1				Sheet 2				Sheet 3			
Participant	C1	C2	C3	C4	C1	C2	C3	C4	C1	C2	C3	C4
pos.1	OK	OK	OK	OK	OK	OK	OK	OK	OK	OK	OK	X
pos.2	OK	OK	OK	OK	OK	OK	OK	OK	OK	OK	OK	X
pos.3	OK	OK	OK	OK	X	X	OK	OK	NE	NE	NE	NE
pos.4	OK	OK	OK	OK	OK	OK	OK	X	OK	OK	X	OK
pos.5	OK	OK	OK	OK	OK	OK	OK	OK	OK	OK	OK	OK
pos.6	OK	X	X	X	OK	OK	OK	OK	OK	OK	OK	X
pos.7	OK	OK	OK	X	OK	OK	OK	OK	NE	NE	NE	NE
pos.8	OK	OK	OK	OK	OK	X	OK	OK	OK	OK	X	X
pos.9	OK	OK	OK	OK	X	OK	OK	OK	OK	OK	OK	OK
pos.10	OK	OK	OK	OK	OK	X	OK	X	OK	OK	X	X

TAB. 6 - POST-TEST EVALUATION

It's worth pointing out that most of the participants - except for participants "pos.2" and "pos.6" - chose to

[7] 1) The participant had to briefly look at the sheet in question and choose whether or not to perform it; 2) If they chose to perform it, they had to read it uninterruptedly; 3) The tempo had to be set by the participant themselves, who had to maintain it until the end of the sheet in question; 4) The use of any form of conducting, whether traditional, or with foot marking, as well as the conducting proposed in the O Passo method, now known, was permitted; 5) The execution could be with claps or other forms of body percussion or even with a phoneme, as well as the oral or body notations proposed in the O Passo method, now known. 6) When finishing a sheet, the same procedures should be carried out with the next one (if there was one).

use the specific regimentation proposed by the O Passo method to carry out the post-test. Based on the data in the table above, we have the following hit margins (See Table 7 - Post-test hit margins).

Post-test	HITS	MARGIN
SHEET 1	37/40	92,5%
SHEET 2	33/40	82,5%
SHEET 3	24/40	60%
TOTAL	**108/120**	**90%**

TAB. 7 - POST-TEST MARGINS OF ACCURACY

It can be seen in this table (see Table 5 - Post-test hit margins) and compared with the pre-test hit margin table (see Table 3 - Pre-test hit margins) that the total hit margin rose from 40% to 90%. From the point of view of the mediation of the method for rhythmic reading at first glance, it proved to be effective, as the participants were able to carry out the tasks during the lessons and in the post-test they demonstrated that: they had developed the skill of rhythmic reading and the other rhythmic skills involved; and they were motivated for this activity and the development of this skill; they experienced positive emotional experiences that provided self-confidence both in their own rhythmic performance and for the teaching of rhythm in their teaching activities.

According to the Self-Determination Theory, when comparing initial motivation with final motivation, the latter seems to have increased in quality as a result of the activities systematised with the O Passo method, which are considered extrinsic factors. In this sense, this learning process generated a motivation that was increasingly intensified and internalised as the classes went on, due to the fact that the participants realised they could do the exercises. In the initial questionnaire, it was noted that there weren't many expectations for the rhythmic reading activities and there were answers without much interest, such as: "it's just another access to the repertoire". Towards the end of the activities with the method, the general motivation of the participants increased greatly in relation to the use of rhythmic activities, to the point that they presented the possibility of working with rhythmic reading even in their teaching activity.

CHAPTER 6

CONCLUSIONS

Taking into account the bibliographical review of this research, it was concluded that music reading: 1) is considered a tool for an individual's musical autonomy; (BOYLE, 1970; CIAVATTA, 2009; FIREMAN, 2007); 2) musicians have different levels of this skill; 3) that reading at first sight is the task that most highlights these differences because it is a "clean" reading, whose primary source of information is the score (visual input) (SLOBODA, 2008). Therefore, the only way to assess the ability to read music in isolation is through an LPV task.

LPV is also considered a complex activity, requiring a large amount of visual information processing and conversion to musical information in real time (LEHMANN AND MCARTHUR, 2002), but mere decoding is not enough, as it needs to have reasonable timing and expression, considering that the interpretation should be as close as possible to a rehearsed performance (OTUTUMI, 2011).

Authors also point out the low relevance given to music reading. Its teaching and training is often neglected by schools and some experts question its necessity, considering that it is not an essential skill for making music (FIREMAN, 2007; HOLLINGSWORTH, 2014). Another issue is that LPV is not taught rigorously nor does it occur so early in children's development, as it is not necessary for full engagement with culture (SLOBODA, 2008).

Due to the complexity of the LPV task and also to the fact that rhythmic reading is its main predictor of performance (BOYLE, 1970; ELLIOT, 1982; BEBEAU, 1982; HODGES, 1992; SHEHAN, 1987; MCPHERSON, 1994) and that rhythmic performance has a highly positive correlation with general musical abilities (HODGES, 1992), the scope of this research was reduced to this reading modality.

Almost all the strategies given by Lehmann and McArthur (2002) for the development of rhythmic reading - such as the use of body movements, the alignment of bars, writing counts in the score and practising together - are bases and tools of the O Passo method. In the method, the group and the body are fundamental for rhythmic execution; body notations are proposed for musical mapping; and the O Passo score provides the alignment of the elements, which includes the use of numbers and phonemes, which is akin to "counting".

Based on the data acquired from the field research carried out, it can be concluded that the O Passo method fulfils its role as a mediator in the development of rhythmic reading at first sight, since the accuracy margins of the participants who took part in the study increased from 40% in the pre-test to 90% in the post-test. These results are consistent with research into the use of body movements to learn to read music (BOYLE, 1970; BEBEAU, 1982; LEHMANN and MCARTHUR, 2002) and also the use of words, numbers, syllables or phonemes in order to decode the traditional score (BEBEAU, 1982; COLLEY, 1987; ESTER, SHEIB AND INKS, 2006).

With regard to the motivation perspective, the answers to the initial questionnaire show that, according to the Self-Determination Theory (DECI and RYAN apud ARAÚJO, 2015), the participants had extrinsic motivations for reading music, classified as external - avoiding punishment and/or obtaining a reward (becoming a teacher, fulfilling the curriculum, etc.), and identified - agreement with the importance of the activity (access to the repertoire, understanding to teach music, etc.).

The answers to the final questionnaire also reflected motivational elements from which it can be deduced, for example, that the participants may have eventually experienced a state of flow through the use of "The Step" method, as their answers about their practice with the method indicated joy, happiness and satisfaction. This can also be explained by considering that the activities with the method were planned with clear objectives and with an appropriate level of difficulty in relation to the participants' skill level. In this sense, the results are consistent with research by Lessa (2015) who studied the state of flow through the application of the "O Passo" method and observed the existence of flow components during the execution of the method, such as involvement, clear goals and feedback, concentration, balance between challenges and skills, etc.

The students' experiences also favoured an increase in their self-efficacy beliefs (BANDURA, 2008), as it was possible to see that the participants had personal experiences of success during the process; they were positively influenced by their classmates through vicarious experiences (observation and comparison with each other); and they also received positive influences from the teacher through verbal persuasion. These factors, therefore, increased the self-efficacy beliefs for the music reading activity and caused the participants to also have an increase in the self-efficacy belief for teaching.

The answers in the final questionnaire, compared to those in the initial questionnaire, also indicate that the motivation for music reading was intensified after the activities with the method, to the point where the participants stated that they would use the O Passo method for teaching music and music reading in their teaching activities.

Finally, it is hoped that this research will provide relevant considerations and data on the development of rhythmic reading at first sight and also on the strategies and tools proposed throughout the literature review, as well as by the experiment itself. It is also hoped to instigate further studies into music reading; sight-reading; rhythmic reading; music education methods that use body movements - especially the O Passo method; as well as studies into motivation for all these music education activities.

REFERENCES

ARAÚJO, R. C. Motivation and Music Teaching. In: Minds in music. Beatriz Senoi Ilari & Rosane Cardoso de Araújo (Orgs.). Curitiba: Ed. UFPR, 2010. p.111-130.

ARAÚJO, R. C. Self-efficacy beliefs and flow theory in music practice, teaching and learning. In:

Revista Percepta, 1(1), pp. 55-66. Brazilian Association of Cognition and Musical Arts, 2013.

ARAÚJO, R. C. Motivation for the practice and learning of music. In: Studies on motivation and emotion in music education. ARAÚJO, R. C. and RAMOS, D. (Orgs.). Curitiba: Editora UFPR, 2015.

ARAÚJO, R. C.; GONÇALVES, L. S. A study on musical perception and self-efficacy beliefs in the context of a higher education institution in Paraná. In: Revista da Abem. Londrina, 2014, v.22, n.33, p. 137 -153.

BANDURA, A. The evolution of social cognitive theory. In: BANDURA, A.; AZZI, R.G.; POLYDORO, S. (Orgs.). Social cognitive theory. Porto Alegre: Artmed, 2008, p. 43-67.

BEBEAU, M. Effects of Traditional and Simplified Methods of Rhythm-Reading Instruction. In: Journal of Research in Music Education. vol. 30, n° 2, pp. 107-119, 1982.

BOYLE, J. David. The Effect of Prescribed Rhythmical Movements on the Ability to Read Music at Sight. In: Journal of Research in Music Education. Vol 18, n° 4, 1970, pp.307-318.

BZUNECK, José A. Motivating your students: always a possible challenge, In.: Psicologia da Educação social network, 2009. Available at: www6.ufrgs.br/psicoeduc/comunidade/action/file/download (last accessed on 29 June 2015).

BZUNECK, José A. Teachers' self-efficacy beliefs. In: Psychology readings for teacher training, 2000. Available at http://mx.leg.ufpr.br/lib/exe/fetch.php/projetos:educacao:bzuneck1.pdf (last accessed on 28 January 2016).

CIAVATTA, L. O Passo: a pulsação e o ensino-aprendizagem de ritmos. Master's dissertation: Fluminense Federal University, Department of Education. Rio de Janeiro: UFF, 2002.

CIAVATTA, L. O Passo: música e educação / Lucas Ciavatta. - Rio de Janeiro: L. Ciavatta, 2009.

COLLEY, B. Comparison of Syllabic Methods for Improving Rhythm Literacy. Journal of Research in Music Education. Vol. 35, No. 4 (Winter, 1987), p. 221-235.

COSTA, J. F. Sight-reading in the training of collaborative pianists from a qualitative approach.

Doctoral thesis. Campinas: UNICAMP Arts Institute, 2011.

ELLIOT, Charles A. The Relationships among Instrumental Sight-Reading Ability and Seven Selected Predictor Variables. In: Journal of Research in Music Education. vol. 30, n° 1, 1982, p. 5-14.

ESTER, D. P., SHEIB; John W. and INKS, K. J. Takadimi: A Rhythm System for All Ages. Music Educators Journal. Vol. 93, No. 2 (Nov., 2006), p. 60-65.

FIREMAN, M. C. Teaching music reading at first sight: suggestions from the research literature. In: Revista Musifal. Alagoas: UFAL, 2007.

FIREMAN, M. C. Reading music at first sight on the guitar: the influence of the organisation of study material. Thesis (Doctorate in Music). Salvador: UFBA, 2010.

GIL, Antônio C. *Métodos e técnicas de pesquisa social.* 5ª ed. São Paulo: Atlas, 2008.

HODGES, D. A. *The acquisition of music-reading skills. In*: R. Colwell (ed.), Handbook of Research in Music Teaching and Learning. New York: Schirmer Books, 1992.

HOLLINGSWORTH, K. J. *The Effects of Length of Instruction on Rhythm-Reading Learning and Retention.* Dissertation for the Degree of Doctor of Philosophy. Alabama: Auburn University, 2014.

KOPIEZ, R.; LEE, J. I.: *Towards a general model of skills involved in sight reading music.* Music Education Research. Hanover: Institute for Research in Music Education, Hanover University of Music and Drama, 2008.

LEEHMAN, A. C.; MCARTHUR, V. *Sight Reading. In*: MCPHERSON, G. E.; PARNCUTT, R. The science and psychology of music performance. New York: Oxford, 2002.

LEEHMAN, A. C.; SLOBODA, J. A.; WOODY, R.H. *Psychology for Musicians: understanding and acquiring skills.* New York: Oxford, 2007.

LESSA, L. *Aspectos motivacionais da aprendizagem musical dos membros da bateria do bloco de carnaval Sargento Pimenta através do método O Passo*: um estudo com base na teoria do fluxo.

Master's dissertation, Federal University of Paraná - Department of Arts. Curitiba: UFPR, 2015.

MCPHERSON, G. E. *Factors and Abilities Influencing Sightreading Skill in Music*. Journal of Research in Music Education, 1994, Vol. 42, No. 3, pp. 217-231.

MCPHERSON, G. E.; O'NEILL, S. A. *Motivation.* In: MCPHERSON, G. E.; PARNCUTT, R. The science and psychology of music performance. New York: Oxford, 2002.

MISHRA, J. Factors Related to Sight-Reading Accuracy: A Meta-Analysis. *Journal of Research in Music Education,* 2014. Vol. 61, No. 4, p. 452 - 455.

OTUTUMI, C. H. V. Initial considerations on sight-reading, memorisation and the discipline of Musical Perception. *In*: *Proceedings of the 5th Embap Academic Guitar Symposium*, 2011.

PERSELLIN, Diane C. Responses to Rhythm Patterns When Presented to Children through Auditory, Visual, and Kinesthetic Modalities. *Journal of Research in Music Education*. 1992, vol. 4, n°4, p. 306-315.

PENTTINEN, M., HUOVINEN, E. The Early Development of Sight-Reading Skills in Adulthood: A Study of Eye Movements. *Journal of Research in Music Education*. 2011, n°59, vol.2, p. 196-220.

SHEHAN, P. Effects of Rote versus Note Presentations on Rhythm Learning and Retention. *Journal of Research in Music Education*, v. 35, n° 2, 1987, pp. 117-126.

SIMÃO, J. P. *Música corporal e o corpo do som:* um estudo dos processos de ensino da percussão corporal do Barbatuques. Master's dissertation, State University of Campinas, Faculty of Education. Campinas: UNICAMP, 2013.

SLOBODA, J. A. *The Musical Mind: The Cognitive Psychology of Music*. Londrina: EDUEL, 2008.

SLOBODA, J. A. *Exploring the Musical Mind.* New York: Oxford, 2004.

WINTER, A.; SINICO, L.L. Anxiety in Musical Performance: definitions, causes, symptoms, strategies and treatments. In: Revista do Conservatório de Música da UFPel, n. 5. Pelotas UFPel, 2012.

ANNEX I - Numbers (time)

Números (tempo)

A	1	(2)	(3)	(4)
B	(1)	(2)	3	(4)
C	(1)	2	(3)	(4)
D	(1)	(2)	(3)	4
E	1	(2)	3	(4)
	(1)	2	(3)	4
F	1	(2)	3	4
	(1)	2	(3)	(4)

(SOURCE: CIAVATTA, 2009)

ANNEX II - e (setback)

e (contratempo)

A	1		2		(3)		(4)	
B	1	e	2		(3)		(4)	
C	1	e	2		3		4	
D	1	e	2		3	e	4	
E	1	e	2	e	3	e	4	
F	1	e	2	e	3	e	4	e
G	(1)	e	(2)	e	(3)	e	(4)	e
H	1	e	(2)	e	(3)	e	(4)	e
I	1		(2)	e	3	e	(4)	e
	(1)	e	2		(3)		4	
J	1		(2)	e	(3)	e	(4)	
	(1)	e	2		3		4	e

(SOURCE: CIAVATTA, 2009)

ANNEX III - Correspondence between scores/Activities with the method

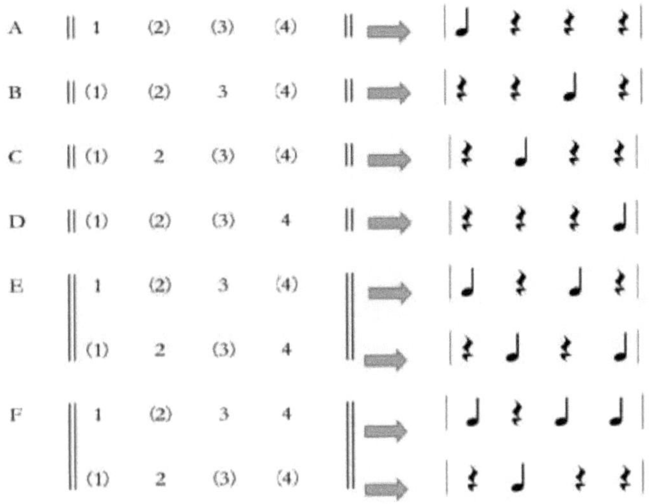

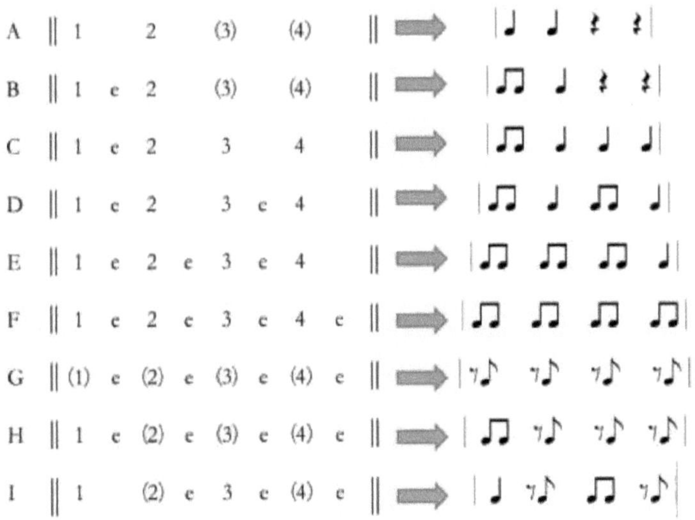

QUESTIONNAIRE ON MUSICAL PRACTICE

Age:

Gender: Male ( ) Female ( )

1) How long have you been studying music?

2) Do you play an instrument? Which one(s)?

3) Are you familiar with musical notation (can you read musical notes and rhythms)?

( ) yes ( ) no ( ) more or less

4) If you answered "yes" or "more or less" to the previous question, please tick the skill(s) below that you have mastered:
   ( ) reading rhythms using musical writing
   ( ) reading musical notes (pitches)

5) Do you think learning to read sheet music (notation) is relevant to musical practice?

( )yes ( )no ( )don't know

Please justify your answer:

ANNEX V - PRE-TEST

(Folha 1)

(Folha 2)

(Folha 3)

ANNEX VI - POST-TEST

(Folha 1)

(Folha 2)

(Folha 3)

ANNEX VII - FINAL QUESTIONNAIRE

FINAL QUESTIONNAIRE

Age:

1) How was your experience with the "O Passo" method during the course? Please point out aspects of this experience, considering the concepts (position, musical space, etc.) and tools (oral notations, body notations and the "O Passo" score, etc.).
2) Do you think the O Passo method can be a tool for learning rhythmic reading?
( ) yes ( ) no ( )don't know

3) After using the "O Passo" method, do you feel more confident about rhythmic reading?
( ) yes ( ) no

4) Would you use "The Step" activities with your students in class?

( )yes ( )no ( )maybe

Justify your answer:

APPENDIX

INFORMED CONSENT FORM

My name is Luiz Carlos Martins Loyola Filho, I'm a student at UFPR, on the Master's programme in Music Education and Cognition, and I'm doing research into methodologies for musical rhythmic practice. This study is part of my master's dissertation, which is being developed under the guidance of Prof Dr Rosane Cardoso de Araújo.

In this regard, I would like to inform you that the participants in the research: (a) will have their identities preserved, as there will be no identification; (b) participation in the research does not cause moral, physical or psychological harm to the participants; (c) participation is free and allows the participant to withdraw if they do not wish to continue.

The research includes two stages. The FIRST STAGE consists of carrying out a pre-test **on music reading and completing an initial questionnaire; and the SECOND STAGE consists of carrying out a** post-test **and completing a final questionnaire.**

I would very much like to count on your collaboration in this research, as your participation is VERY IMPORTANT for its realisation!

To confirm your participation, please sign this document in the space below.

Thank you very much,

Luiz Carlos Martins Loyola Filho

I AGREE TO TAKE PART IN THE RESEARCH: ________________________________

DATE AND PLACE: Curitiba, ___ of ______________________________ 2015

MIX
Papier aus verantwortungsvollen Quellen
Paper from responsible sources
FSC® C105338

FSC
www.fsc.org

Printed by Books on Demand GmbH, Norderstedt / Germany